Albert Schweitzer is known throughout the world as a great humanitarian: physician, philosopher, musician, and theologian. In addition to his extraordinary work at the Lambaréné hospital in Equatorial Africa, he also keeps up his organ technique on a specially equipped piano, writes deeply perceptive books, and gives lectures and recitals to raise funds for his hospital. His profound nobility of spirit and reverence for life are vividly portrayed in his inspiring autobiography, *Out of my Life and Thought*.

Peace
or
Atomic War?

Three appeals broadcast from Oslo, Norway,
on April 28, 29, and 30, 1958

Peace

or

Atomic War?

by

ALBERT SCHWEITZER

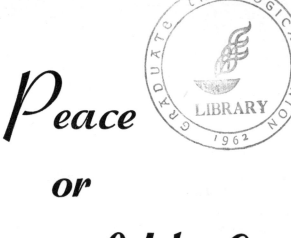

HENRY HOLT AND COMPANY   NEW YORK

87757-0218

Printed in the United States of America

One

The Renunciation of Nuclear Tests

IN APRIL of 1957, I raised my voice, together with others, to draw attention to the great danger of radioactive poisoning of the air and the earth, following tests with atom (uranium) bombs and hydrogen bombs. With others I appealed to the nuclear powers to come to an agreement to stop the tests as soon as possible, while declaring their genuine desire to renounce the use of atomic weapons.

At the time there was reasonable hope that this step would be taken. It was not to be. The 1957 negotiations in London that summer, led by Mr. Harold Stassen of the United States, achieved nothing. The conference arranged by the United Nations in the autumn of that year suffered the same fate through the withdrawal of the Soviet Union from the discussions.

The Soviet Union has recently made a disarmament proposal on the basis of which discussions are apparently being planned. As a first step the plan presupposes that nuclear tests should cease immediately.

What chances has this condition of being fulfilled?

It might be thought that it would be easy for all those involved to reach agreement on this point. None of

9

them would have to sacrifice any of the atomic weapons in their possession, while the handicap of not being able to try out new ones would be the same for all.

Even so, the proposal is difficult for the United States and Britain to accept. They spoke against it when the matter was discussed in the spring of 1957. Since then ceaseless propaganda has claimed that the radiation following nuclear tests is so dangerous that it is necessary to stop them. The American and European press is constantly receiving abundant propaganda material supplied by government atomic commissions and scientists who feel called upon to support this view.

From a statement issued by the subcommittee of the American Atomic Energy Commission, I quote the following phrases:

Within the framework of scientific and military requirements, it is advisable that nuclear tests are limited to a minimum. The necessary steps should be taken to correct the present confusion of the general public. The present and potential effects on heredity from the gradual increase in radioactivity of the air are kept within tolerable limits. The possibility of a harmful effect which people believe to be beyond control, has a strong emotional effect. The continuation of nuclear tests is necessary and justified in the interests of national security.

What is meant by "the confusion of the public" is the

fact that people are becoming increasingly aware of dangers resulting from nuclear tests.

The probable reasoning behind the obscure statement that the "effects on heredity from the gradual increase in radioactivity of the air are kept within tolerable limits" is that the number of children who will be born deformed—as a result of the harm done to the sexual cells—supposedly will not be large enough to justify the stopping of the tests.

The view of the scientists who feel called upon to reduce the danger of radioactivity to what they believe to be its right proportions is expressed by a Central European scientist who concluded a speech on this subject with the following bold, prophetic words:

If the tests are carried on with the same frequency as in the last few years, the radioactive poisoning will be four times stronger in 1983 than at present, and about six times stronger around the year 2010. Even that strength would be small compared with natural radiation. It can be stated categorically that the risk for mankind involved in nuclear tests is small. That is not to say that there is no risk. In this context I should like to quote the words of the American physicist and member of the Atomic Energy Commission, Dr. Libby: 'The risk of radioactive poisoning must be balanced against the risk to which the entire free world would be exposed if nuclear tests were abandoned before a safe international disarmament agreement has been brought about. The tests are necessary if the United States is not to be left behind in the development of nuclear weapons.'

During the continued reassurance campaign a very prominent American nuclear physicist went to the length of declaring that the total number of luminous watch dials in the world represents a greater danger than the radioactive fall-out of nuclear tests up till now.

The reassurance propaganda expects much from the glad tidings that science has succeeded in making the prototype of a hydrogen bomb producing far less of dangerous radioactive materials than the usual ones. The new bomb is called "the clean hydrogen bomb". The old type must from now on be content to be called the dirty bomb.

The clean hydrogen bomb differs from the other in having a jacket made of a material which does not, like Uranium 238, release immense quantities of radioactive elements at the enormous explosive temperature. That is why it is less harmful as regards radioactivity. It is also, however, less powerful.

The new, highly praised hydrogen bomb is—let it be said in passing—only relatively clean. Its trigger is a uranium bomb made of the fissionable Uranium 235— an atomic bomb as powerful as the one dropped over Hiroshima. This bomb, when detonated, also produces radioactivity, as do the neutrons released in great numbers at the explosion.

In an American newspaper at the beginning of this

year, Dr. Edward Teller, the father of the dirty hydrogen bomb, sang a hymn of praise to the idyllic nuclear war to be waged with completely clean hydrogen bombs. He insists on a continuation of the tests, to perfect this ideal bomb: "Further tests will put us in a position to fight our opponents' war machine, while sparing the innocent bystanders. Clean weapons of this kind will reduce unnecessary casualties in a future war."

Of course, neither the United States nor the Soviet Union is thinking of producing this less effective bomb for use in a possible war. The U. S. Department of Defense has quite recently declared that the irradiation of whole areas has become a new offensive weapon.

The clean hydrogen bomb is intended for window display only, not for use. The bomb is to encourage people to believe that future nuclear tests will be followed by less and less radiation, and that there is no argument against the continuation of the tests.

Those who think that the danger created by nuclear tests is small mainly take air radiation into consideration, persuading themselves that the danger limit has not yet been reached.

The results of their arithmetic are, however, not so reliable as they would like to believe. Through the years the toleration limit for radiation had to be reduced several times. In 1934, it was 100 radiation units per year. At present the limit is officially put at five. In many countries it is even lower. Dr. Lauriston Taylor

(U.S.A.), who is regarded as an authority on protection against radiation, holds with others that it is an open question whether there is anything called a harmless amount of radiation. He thinks that we can only speak of an amount of radiation which we regard as tolerable.

We are constantly being told about "a permissible amount of radiation." Who permitted it? Who has any right to permit it?

When speaking about the risk of radiation we must take into consideration not only the radiation coming from the outside, but also that coming from radioactive elements in our body.

What is the source of this radioactivity?

The radioactive elements released in the air by nuclear tests do not stay there permanently. In the form of radioactive rain and radioactive snow they fall down on the earth. They enter the plants through leaves and roots and stay there. We absorb them through the plants by drinking milk from the cows or by eating the meat of animals which have fed on them. Radioactive rain infects our drinking water.

The most powerful radioactive poisoning occurs in the areas between the Northern latitudes 10° and 60°, because of the numerous nuclear tests conducted mainly in these latitudes by the Soviet Union and the United States.

The radioactive elements absorbed over the years by our bodies are not evenly distributed in the cellular tissue, but are deposited and accumulated at certain points. From these points the internal radiation takes place, causing injuries to particularly vulnerable organs. What this kind of radiation lacks in strength is made up for by its persistence, working as it does day and night for years.

It is a well-known fact that one of the most widespread and dangerous elements absorbed by us is Strontium 90. It is stored in the bones and from there emits its rays into cells of red bone marrow, where the red and white corpuscles are made. Blood diseases— fatal in most cases—are the result. The cells of the reproductive organs are particularly sensitive to this element. Even relatively weak radiation may lead to fatal consequences.

The most sinister aspect of both internal and external radiation is that years may pass before the evil consequences appear. Indeed, they make themselves felt, not in the first nor second generation, but in the following ones. Generation after generation, for centuries to come, will witness the birth of an ever-increasing number of children with mental and physical defects.

It is not for the physicist, choosing to take into account only the radiation from the air, to say the decisive word on the dangers of nuclear tests. That right belongs to the biologists and physicians who have studied internal as well as external radiation, and those physicists who pay attention to the facts established by the biologists and physicians.

The declaration signed by 9,235 scientists of all nations, handed to the Secretary General of the United

Nations by the renowned American scientist, Dr. Linus Pauling, on January 13, 1958, gave the reassurance propaganda its deathblow. The scientists declared that the radioactivity gradually created by nuclear tests represents a greater danger for all parts of the world and is particularly serious because its consequence will be an increasing number of deformed children in the future. For this reason they demanded an international agreement puting an end to the nuclear tests.

Propaganda for the continuation of nuclear tests can no longer maintain that the scientists do not agree on the question of the danger of radiation, and that one must, therefore, await the decision of international bodies and abstain from alarming the public by saying that radiation represents an actual danger growing more serious every day.

This propaganda will continue to set the tone in certain newspapers. But beside it the truth about the danger of nuclear tests marches imperturbably along, influencing an ever-increasing section of public opinion. In the long run, even the most efficiently organized propaganda can do nothing against the truth.

One incomprehensible aspect of the propaganda for the continuation of nuclear tests is its complete disregard of their harmful effects on future generations which, according to biologists and physicians, will be the result of the radiation to which we are being exposed.

The declaration signed by the 9,235 scientists did well in stressing the danger.

We must not be responsible for the future birth of thousands of children with the most serious mental and physical defects simply because we did not pay enough attention to that danger. Only those who have never been present at the birth of a deformed baby, never witnessed the despair of its mother, dare to maintain that the risk in going on with nuclear tests is one which must be taken under existing circumstances. The well-known French biologist and geneticist, Jean Rostand, calls the continuation of nuclear tests *"le crime dans l'avenir"* (the crime projected into the future). It is the particular duty of women to prevent this sin against the future. It is for them to raise their voices against it in such a way that they will be heard.

It is strange that so far nobody has stressed that the question of whether nuclear tests should be stopped or continued is not one which concerns the nuclear powers exclusively. Who is giving these countries the right to experiment, in time of peace, with weapons involving the most serious risks for the whole world? What has international law—enthroned by the United Nations and so highly praised in our time—to say on this matter? Does it no longer look out on the world from its ivory tower? Then it must be brought back into the world again so that it may face the facts and do its duty accordingly.

International law would at once discover the deplorable case of Japan, which suffers heavily from the effects

of nuclear tests. The radioactive clouds created by the
Soviet tests in Northeast Siberia and by the American
ones at Bikini in the Pacific Ocean are carried by the
winds over Japan. The resulting radioactive poisoning
is the worst possible. Very heavy radioactive rainfalls
are quite common. The radioactive poisoning of the soil
and the vegetation is so powerful that the inhabitants
of various districts ought to abstain from using their
harvest for food. But they have no alternative but to eat
rice infected with strontium, an element particularly
dangerous to children. The ocean surrounding Japan is
also at times dangerously radioactive, and thereby the
very food supply of the country—in which fish has
always played an important part—is being threatened
because of the large amount of radioactive fish unsuit-
able for consumption.

As every new nuclear test makes a bad situation
worse, the Japanese Government, when hearing of plans
for new tests to the north or south of Japan, has pre-
sented its country's urgent appeal in Washington or
Moscow, beseeching the American or Soviet authorities
to give up their plans. The answer was always the same
—they regretted there could be no question of doing so
while as yet the powers had not reached an agreement
to that effect. As recently as February 20, 1958, this
happened again in the capital of one of the nuclear
powers.

We always learn about such appeals and their refusal
through short paragraphs in the newspaper—just like
any other news item. The press does not disturb us with

editorials drawing our attention to and making us share in what lies behind such news—the misery of the Japanese people. Thus we and the press are guilty of a lack of compassion. More guilty however is international law, which has kept silent and indifferent on this question year after year.

It is high time to realize that the question of continuing or ceasing nuclear tests is an urgent matter for international law. Mankind is imperiled by the tests. Mankind insists that they stop, and has every right to do so.

If there is left in the civilization of our times anything of living international law, or if it should be re-established, then the nations responsible for nuclear tests must renounce them immediately, without making this dependent on a disarmament agreement. This matter has nothing to do with disarmament. The nations in question will continue to keep those weapons which they now have.

There is no time to lose. New tests increasing the danger must not be allowed to take place. It is important to realize that even without new tests the danger will increase during the coming years: a large part of the radioactive elements flung up in the atmosphere and stratosphere during the nuclear experiments is still there. It will come down only after several years, probably about fifteen.

The immediate renunciation of further tests will create a favorable atmosphere for talks on banning the use of nuclear weapons. When this urgently necessary step has been taken, such negotiations can take place in peace.

That the Soviet Union is now willing to renounce further tests is of great importance. If Britain and the United States could bring themselves to the same reasonable decision demanded by international law, humanity would be liberated from the fear of being threatened in its existence by the increase of the radioactive poisoning of the air and of the soil resulting from the tests.

Two

The Danger of an Atomic War

TODAY WE HAVE to envisage the menacing possibility of an outbreak of atomic war between Soviet Russia and the United States. It can only be avoided if the two powers decide to renounce atomic arms.

How has this situation arisen?

In 1945, the United States produced an atom bomb with Uranium 235. On August 6, 1945, this bomb was released on Hiroshima, and on August 9, on Nagasaki.

America's possession of such a bomb gave her a military advantage over other countries.

In July, 1949, the Soviet Union also possessed such a bomb. And its power was equal to the one which was brought into being by America between 1946 and 1949. Consequently peace between the two powers was maintained on the basis of mutual respect for the other country's bomb.

On October 3, 1952, England exploded its first atom bomb on the Isle of Montebello, on the northwest coast of Australia.

Then, to secure an advantage, the United States made the decision to invite Dr. Edward Teller to produce the hydrogen bomb. It was expected that this H-bomb would exceed many times the power of the uranium bomb. This bomb was first released in May, 1951, at Eniwetok on the Pacific atoll, Elugelab, in October, 1952. On March 1, 1954, at Bikini, one of the group in the Marshall Islands in the Pacific Ocean, the perfected H-bomb was exploded. It was found that the actual power of the explosion was much stronger than was originally expected on the basis of calculations.

But at the same time as the United States, the Soviet Union also started producing H-bombs, the first of which was exploded on August 12, 1953. Both powers progressed contemporaneously. (The United States invented the atom bomb during the Second World War, and subsequently worked on the principles of the rockets which served Germany in those days.)

War no longer depends on the ability of mighty airplanes to carry bombs to their targets. Now there are guided rockets that can be launched from their starting point and directed with accuracy to a distant target. Missiles are carried by such rockets propelled by a fuel which is constantly being developed in efficiency. The missile carried by the rocket can be an ordinary missile or one which contains a uranium warhead or an H-bomb warhead.

It is said that the Soviet Union has rockets with a range of up to 625 miles, and with a probable range of up to 1,100 miles.

The United States is said to possess rockets with a range of 1,500 miles.

Whether the so-called intercontinental missile with a range of 5,000 miles exists, cannot be ascertained. It is assumed that the problem of its production is on the way to being solved, and that both East and West are occupied with its production.

Although an intercontinental rocket is not yet known to be completed, America has to be prepared for submarines shooting such a projectile far into the country. These rockets proceed with immense velocity. It is expected that an intercontinental rocket would not take more than half an hour to cross the ocean with bomb-loads of from one to five tons.

How would an atomic war be conducted today? At first the so-called local war—but today there is little difference between a local war and a global war. Rocket missiles will be used up to a range of 1,500 miles. The destruction should not be underestimated, even if caused only by a Hiroshima-type bomb, not to speak of an H-bomb.

It can hardly be expected that an enemy will renounce the use of atom bombs, or the most perfected H-bombs, on large cities from the very outset. The H-bomb has a thousandfold stronger development of power than the atom bomb.

It is therefore quite possible that in a future atomic war both rocket projectiles and large bombers will be used together. Rocket projectiles will not replace bombers, but will rather complement them.

The immediate effect of an H-bomb will have a range of several miles. The heat will be 100 million degrees.

One can imagine how great would be the number of city-dwellers destroyed by the pressure of the explosion, by flying fragments of glass, by heat and fire, and by radioactive waves, even if the attack were only of short duration. The deadly radioactive infection, as a consequence of the explosion, would have a range of some 45,000 square miles.

A United States general said to some congressmen: "If at intervals of ten minutes, one hundred and ten H-bombs are dropped over the U.S.A. there would be a casualty list of about seventy million people, besides some thousands of square miles made useless for a whole generation. Countries like England, West Germany, and France could be finished off with fifteen to twenty H-bombs."

President Eisenhower has pointed out, after watching maneuvers under atomic attack, that defense measures in a future atomic war become useless. In these circumstances all one can do is to pray.

Indeed, not much more can be done in view of an attack by H-bombs than to advise everyone to hide behind very strong walls of stone or cement, and to throw themselves on the ground, and to cover the back of their heads and the body, if possible, with cloth. In this way it might be possible to escape annihilation and death through radiation. It would be essential that those surviving be given food and drink which were not radioactive and that they be transported away from the radioactive district.

It is impossible to erect walls of such thickness for the whole population of a city. Where would the material and the means come from? How would a population even have time to run to safety in such bunkers?

In an atomic war there would be neither conqueror nor vanquished. During such a bombardment both sides would suffer the same fate. A continuous destruction would take place and no armistice nor peace proposals could bring it to an end.

When people deal with atomic weapons, no one could say to the other, "Now the arms must decide"; but only, "Now we want to commit suicide together, destroying each other mutually. . . ."

An English M.P. has said with good reason, "He who uses atomic weapons becomes subject to the fate of a bee, namely, when it stings it will perish inevitably for having made use of its sting." He who uses atomic weapons to defend freedom would become subject to a similar fate.

Those who conduct an atomic war for freedom will die, or end their lives miserably. Instead of freedom they will find destruction. Radioactive clouds resulting from a war between East and West would imperil humanity everywhere. There would be no need to use up the remaining stock of atom and H-bombs. (There are about 50,000 of them.)

An atomic war is therefore the most senseless and lunatic act that could ever take place. At all costs it must be prevented.

Unfortunately a cold war may turn into an atomic war. This danger is made greater today than it has ever been because of the possibility of employing long-distance rockets.

In the past, the United States held to the principle of being, apart from the Soviet Union, the sole owner of atomic weapons. There was no virtue in equipping other countries with atom and H-bombs, for they would not have known what to do with them. But, with the arrival of rocket projectiles of a smaller type and a longer range, the situation is changing. The use of such smaller weapons is possible for lesser countries who are in alliance with America. Thus the United States has deviated from her principle of not putting atomic weapons into the hands of other countries, a decision which carries grave consequences.

On the other hand it is understandable that America wishes to supply the NATO countries with such new weapons for defense against the Soviet Union. The presence of such arms constitutes a new threat to the Soviet Union, opening the way for an atomic war between the United States and the Soviet Union on European soil. This situation did not exist before. Now the Soviet Union is within range of such rockets from European soil—even as far as Moscow and Kharkov—up to 1,500 miles away.

Rockets of average range could be used for defense purposes by Turkey and Iran against the Soviet Union, into which they could penetrate deeply with such arms accepted from America, and the Soviet Union in turn might be forced into a situation in which it had to defend itself.

Both the United States and the Soviet Union may now seek alliances with the Middle East by offering such countries financial support. Any quarrels that might occur could start in secret; unknown events in the Middle East could endanger the peace of the world.

The risk of an atomic war is being increased by the fact that no warning would be given in starting such a war, which could originate in some mere incident. The side that attacks first would have the initial advantage over the attacked, which would at once sustain losses that would reduce its fighting capacity considerably.

The necessity for a round-the-clock alert against attack carries with it the extreme danger of an error in interpreting what appears on a radar screen, when immediate action is imperative, resulting in the outbreak of an atomic war.

Attention was drawn to this danger by the American General Curtis Le May, when the world was recently on the brink of such a situation. The radar stations of the U. S. Air Force and U. S. Coastal Command reported that an invasion of unidentified bombers was on the way. Upon this warning the General, who was in command of the strategic bomber force, decided to order a reprisal bombardment to commence. However, realizing the enormity of his responsibility, he then hesitated. Shortly afterward it was discovered that the radar stations had made a technical error. What would have

happened if a less balanced general had been in his
place?

In the future such dangers are likely to increase owing
to the fact that small rockets exist which pass through
the air with terrific speed and are difficult to identify,
so that defense possibilities become very limited. The
defense has only seconds in which to identify the ap-
proaching rockets and to counterattack by exploding
these before they can reach their targets, and at the
same time dispatch bombers to destroy the ramps from
which they were launched.

Such decisions cannot be left to the human brain, for
it works too slowly. They have to be entrusted to an
electronic brain. If it appears on the radar screen that
enemy rockets are really on the way, calculations as
to their distance have to be made to the fraction of a
second, so that an immediate start can be made by
releasing defense rockets.

All this proceeds automatically. Such is our achieve-
ment that we now depend entirely on an electronic
brain, and on errors and omissions from which such an
instrument cannot be exempt. The making of a decision
by means of an electronic brain, though quicker, is not
so reliable as the making of a decision by the human
brain. At some point the complex mechanism of the
electronic brain may become faulty.

These developments lead inevitably to a worsening of
the situation. We have to reckon with the fact that the

United States may proceed with the supply of atomic weapons to other countries, trusting them not to use them selfishly or incautiously. The two other atomic powers are at liberty to do likewise.

Yet, who can guarantee that among the favored countries in possession of such weapons there may not be black sheep acting on their own, without regard for the consequences? Who is to prevent them? Who is able to make them renounce the use of atomic weapons, even if other countries have decided to make such a decision in common? The dam is breached and it may collapse.

That such anxieties have become very real is shown by a statement on January 13, 1958, on behalf of 9,235 UNO scientists regarding the cessation of atomic tests. One of their points is the following:

> As long as atomic weapons remain in the hands of the three great powers, an agreement as to their control is possible. However, if the tests continue and extend to other countries in possession of atomic weapons, the risks and responsibilities in regard to an outbreak of an atomic war become all the greater. From every point of view the danger in a future atomic war becomes all the more intense, so that an urgent renunciation of atomic weapons becomes absolutely imperative.

The United States' attitude to the renunciation of atomic weapons is remarkable. It cannot be otherwise— her conviction is that they should be outlawed, yet at the same time in case this does not come about she strives with other NATO countries to put herself in the most favorable military situation. Thus America insists that the rockets which she offers to other countries should be accepted as soon as possible. She seeks to hold such a position to enable her to maintain peace by terrifying her opponent. But she is finding that most of the NATO countries are reluctant to acquire the weapons which they are being offered, because of an increasing strengthening of adverse public opinion.

It would be of immense importance if the United States in this hour of destiny could decide in favor of renouncing atomic weapons to remove the possibility of an eventual outbreak of an atomic war. The theory of peace through terrifying an opponent by a greater armament can now only heighten the danger of war.

A ray of light in darkness—in December, 1957, the Polish Foreign Minister, Rapacki, made the proposition that Czechoslovakia, East and West Germany should consist of an atom-free zone. If this proposal is accepted and the atom-free zones could be enlarged to include adjoining countries the maintenance of peace would be assured. The beginning of the end of the specter that overshadows the Soviet Union would become an accomplished fact.

With this sensible proposition, public opinion in Europe is in absolute agreement. It has become convinced, during recent months, that under no circumstances is Europe to become a battlefield for an atomic war between the Soviet Union and the United States. From this conviction it will no longer deviate. The time is past when a European country could plan secretly to establish itself as a great power by manufacturing atomic weapons exclusively for its own use. Since public opinion would never agree to such an undertaking, it becomes senseless even to prepare secretly for the realization of such a plan.

Past, too, is the time when NATO generals and European governments can decide on the establishment of launching sites and the stockpiling of atomic weapons. The dangers of atomic war and its consequences are now such that these decisions have ceased to be purely matters of politics and can be valid only with the sanction of public opinion.

Three

Negotiations at the Highest Level

WHAT IS THE POSITION regarding the negotiations that should lead to the renunciation of nuclear weapons?

One reads and hears that the success of the projected Summit Conference must depend entirely on its every detail being diplomatically prepared beforehand. The best diplomacy is objectivity. A fitting preparation would be in sight (if a respectful and well-meaning criticism is permissible) if the statesmen and others associated with it would change from their present undiplomatic way of dealing with each other and return to a diplomatic method. Many unnecessary, thoughtless, discourteous, foolish, and offensive remarks have passed between them, both in the spoken and written word, to the disadvantage of the political atmosphere.

It would be right if, at last, those who have the authority to take the responsibility—and not those who have only nominal authority and who cannot move an inch beyond their instructions—would confer together.

It would be right to go ahead with the conference. For close on four months, East and West have talked and written to one another without any conclusions as to reaching a specific date or program. Public opinion everywhere is finding it difficult to accept this state of affairs and is beginning to ask itself whether a conference which limps into being has any hope of really achieving anything.

It would be right to hold the conference in a town in some neutral European country, for example, Geneva, as was the case in 1955.

It would be right that at this conference only questions that have to do directly with the renunciation of nuclear weapons should be discussed.

It would be right if not too many people were present at the Summit meeting. Only the highest personalities of the three nuclear powers, together with their experts and advisers, should take their seats there.

Admission could also be permitted to the representatives of those peoples who—like the NATO countries associated with America—are concerned in nuclear matters; they could then state their opinion on the decisions that also hold such grave consequences for them.

It would only be in a quite arbitrary manner that other peoples could claim to be present at the Summit. Either all would be qualified to be there—or none. In addition, experience teaches us that unnecessarily large attendance brings no advantage to a conference.

The Summit Conference, therefore, is in no way an international or half-international one, even though its decisions are of great importance to the whole of mankind.

The three nuclear powers and they alone must decide, in awareness of their responsibility to their peoples and to all mankind, whether or not they will renounce the testing and the use of nuclear weapons.

As to the planning of the conference, impartiality justifies one remark, which is that to date such planning has been done without objectiveness, and has therefore led nowhere. This leads to the thought that the same outcome could result from the Summit Conference if it were conducted in the same manner.

Wherein lies the difference between the partial and the impartial, the fitting and the unfitting in this matter? It lies in the answer to the question as to the basis on which the three nuclear powers decide whether or not to renounce the testing and the use of nuclear weapons.

The unobjective reply would be that the decision will depend on whether an agreement is reached on disarmament or not. This is false logic. It presumes that there could be an agreement acceptable to both the East and the West on this issue. But previous negotiations have shown that this is not to be expected; they got stuck right at the start because East and West were unable to reach agreement even on the conditions under which such discussions should take place.

The anticipated procedure itself by its very nature is not impartial. It is based on false logic. The two vital issues so essential to the very existence of mankind— the cessation of tests and the disposal of nuclear weapons—cannot be made dependent on the Heavens' performing the impossible political miracle that alone could ensure that none of the three nuclear powers would have some objection to a complete agreement on disarmament.

The fact is that the testing and the use of nuclear weapons carry in themselves the absolute reasons for being renounced. Prior agreement on any other conditions cannot be considered. Both cause the deepest damage to human rights. The tests, in that they do harm to peoples far from the territories of the nuclear powers and endanger their lives and their health—and this in peacetime; an atomic war, in that the resulting radioactivity would make uninhabitable the land of peoples not participating in such a war. It would be the most unimaginably senseless and cruel way of endangering the existence of mankind. That is why it dare not become reality.

The three nuclear powers owe it to themselves and to mankind to reach agreement on these absolute essentials without first dealing with prior conditions.

The negotiations about disarmament are therefore not the forerunner of such agreement, but the outcome of it. They start from the point where agreement on the nuclear issues has been reached, and their goal is to reach the point where the three nuclear powers and the peoples who are connected with them must agree on guarantees that will seek to avert the danger of a threat of a nonatomic nature's taking the place of the previous danger. Everything that the diplomats will have done objectively to prepare the preliminaries to the conference will keep its meaning even if it will be used not before renunciation, but as the result of it.

Should agreement be reached on the outlawing of nuclear weapons, this alone without any negotiations will have led to a great improvement in the political situation; as a result of such an agreement, time and distance would again become realities with their own rights. Nuclear arms give a distant war the effect of a near war. The Soviet Union and the United States, in spite of the vast distance that separates them, can menace one another with atomic missiles in such a frightful manner and in such a short space of time as though they adjoined each other. Having become neighbors, they are in constant fear of their lives every minute.

But if nuclear arms were no longer in question, the rockets and missiles would not present nearly the same destructive danger. The nearness that endangers existence would have ceased to be. If rockets are no longer nuclear arms, Europe is no longer a battlefield for a distant war which has the effect of a near war between the Soviet Union and the United States.

Today the United States with her batteries of nuclear rockets is represented as a mighty military power in Europe. Europe has become an in-between land between America and Russia, as if America by some displacement of a continent had come closer to her. But if atomic rockets were no longer in question, this unnatural state of affairs would come to an end. America would again become wholly America; Europe wholly Europe; the Atlantic again wholly the Atlantic Ocean.

In this way the beginning of the end of the United

States' military presence in Europe could come about—
a presence which has arisen from the two World Wars.
The great sacrifices that the United States made for
Europe during the Second World War, and in the years
following it, will not be forgotten; the great and varied
help that Europe received from her, and the thanks
owing for this, will not be forgotten. But the unnatural
situation created by the two World Wars that led to a
dominating military presence in Europe cannot continue indefinitely. It must gradually cease to exist, both
for the sake of Europe and for the sake of America.

Now there will be shocked voices from all sides. What
will become of poor Europe if American atomic weapons no longer defend it from within and from without?
What will happen if Europe is delivered to the Soviets?
Must it then not be prepared to languish in a Com-
munist-Babylonian form of imprisonment for long
years?

Here it should be said that perhaps the Soviet Union
is not quite so malicious as to think only of throwing
itself on Europe at the first opportunity in order to
devour it, and perhaps not quite so unintelligent as to
fail to consider whether there would be any advantage
in upsetting her stomach with this indigestible meal.

What Europe and the Europeans have to agree about
is that they belong together for better or for worse. This
is a new historical fact that can no longer be bypassed
politically.

Another factor that must be recognized politically is
that the question is no longer one of subjugating peo-

ples, but of learning to get along with them mentally and spiritually. A Europe standing on its own has no reason to despair.

Disarmament discussions between the three nuclear powers must concern themselves with guarantees that actual, total, and irrevocable disposal of nuclear weapons will be secured. The problem of effective control will also have to be anticipated. Reciprocal agreement will have to be reached on permitting international commissions to investigate on national soil.

One talks of giving aircraft belonging to an international police force the right to fly at medium and high altitudes for purposes of spying. One asks to what extent a land would be willing to subject itself to such control over its own territory. Unfortunate incidents could easily occur. And what about the power that should be entrusted to such an international control? Even the furthest-reaching international control would not be able to give the assurance that in every country and in all agreements this trust will be fulfilled. In the final analysis East and West are dependent on presupposing a certain reciprocal trust in one another.

This applies also in another matter. As a result of renouncing nuclear arms, the Soviet Union's military might, so far as Europe is concerned, would be less affected than that of the United States. There would remain to the Soviet the many divisions armed with conventional weapons; with those divisions it could easily overrun the NATO states in Western Europe—particularly Western Germany—without it being possible for anyone to come to their aid. With this in mind, the Soviet Union should agree in the course of disarmament negotiations to reduce her army, and to commit herself never to move against Germany. But here, too, no manner of detailed agreements and internationally guaranteed disarmament agreements would be enough; the parties concerned are still dependent on trusting one another.

But we live in a time when the good faith of peoples is doubted more than ever before. Expressions throwing doubt on the trustworthiness of each other are bandied back and forth. They are based on what happened in the First World War when the nations experienced dishonesty, injustice, and inhumanity from one another. How can a new trust come about? And yet, it must.

We cannot continue in this paralyzing mistrust. If we want to work our way out of the desperate situation in which we find ourselves, another spirit must enter into the people. It can only come if the awareness of its necessity suffices to give us strength to believe in its coming. We must presuppose the awareness of this need in all the peoples who have suffered along with us. We must approach them in the spirit that we are human beings, all of us, and that we feel ourselves fitted to feel with each other; to think and to will together in the same way.

The awareness that we are all human beings together has become lost in war and through politics.

We have reached the point of regarding each other only as members of a people either allied with us or against us and our approach: prejudice, sympathy, or antipathy are all conditioned by that. Now we must rediscover the fact that we—all together—are human beings, and that we must strive to concede to each other what moral capacity we have. Only in this way can we begin to believe that in other peoples as well as in ourselves there will arise the need for a new spirit which can be the beginning of a feeling of mutual trustworthiness toward each other. The spirit is a mighty force for transforming things. We have seen it at work as the spirit of evil which virtually threw us back from striving toward a culture of the spirit into barbarism. Now let us set our hopes on the spirit's bringing peoples and nations back to an awareness of culture.

At this stage we have the choice of two risks: the one lies in continuing the mad atomic-arms race with its danger of an unavoidable atomic war in the near future; the other in the renunciation of nuclear weapons, and in the hope that the United States and the Soviet Union, and the peoples associated with them, will manage to live in peace. The first holds no hope of a prosperous future; the second does. We must risk the second.

In President Eisenhower's speech of November 7, 1957, a few days after the launching of Sputnik II, he said, "What the world needs more than a gigantic leap into space is a gigantic leap into peace." This gigantic leap consists in finding the courage to hope that the spirit of good sense will arise in individuals and in peoples, a spirit sufficiently strong to overcome the insanity and the inhumanity.

If negotiations on disarmament are held, not as a preliminary to the renunciation of nuclear arms but as a result of it, they would have a much larger meaning. They would be a big step in the direction of finally liquidating the confused situation that followed the Second World War.

Disarmament and all questions leading to a stable situation—for example, the reunification of East and West Germany—could be discussed much better after agreement had been reached on the renunciation of atomic weapons. A later conference could also deal with many issues left unresolved in the peace treaties after the Second World War.

Once agreement on renunciation of nuclear arms had been reached it would be the responsibility of the United Nations to ensure that now as in the future they would be neither made nor used. The danger that one nation or another might hit on the idea of manufacturing nuclear weapons will have to be borne in mind for some considerable time. We must consider ourselves lucky that they are not yet in the possession of other peoples elsewhere in the world.

The problem of how far disarmament and renunciation of all weapons can go will have to be investigated, because the Second World War showed what terrible destruction conventional weapons can cause, destruction which the development of rockets has potentially vastly increased. One wishes that agreement could be reached immediately to renounce rockets and missiles, but this can only come as a result of a spiritual advance everywhere which as yet it is difficult to visualize.

Of all the very difficult problems the future holds, the most difficult will be the rights of access of over-populated countries to neighboring lands. But if in our time we renounce nuclear arms we shall have taken the first step on the way to the distant goal of the end to all wars. If we do not do this we remain on the road that leads in the near future to atomic war and misery.

Those who are to meet at the Summit must be aware of this, so that they can negotiate with propriety, with an adequate degree of seriousness, and with a full sense of responsibility. The Summit Conference must not fail: mankind will not again tolerate failure. The renunciation of nuclear weapons is vital to peace.

DATE DUE
